Shadows, Memories, and Dreams

Shadows, Memories, and Dreams

A Collection of Ethereal Poetry

ANNIKA DEV

RESOURCE *Publications* • Eugene, Oregon

SHADOWS, MEMORIES, AND DREAMS
A Collection of Ethereal Poetry

Copyright © 2024 Annika Dev. All rights reserved. Except for brief quotations in critical publications or reviews, no part of this book may be reproduced in any manner without prior written permission from the publisher. Write: Permissions, Wipf and Stock Publishers, 199 W. 8th Ave., Suite 3, Eugene, OR 97401.

Resource Publications
An Imprint of Wipf and Stock Publishers
199 W. 8th Ave., Suite 3
Eugene, OR 97401

www.wipfandstock.com

PAPERBACK ISBN: 979-8-3852-0739-8
HARDCOVER ISBN: 979-8-3852-0740-4
EBOOK ISBN: 979-8-3852-0741-1

01/22/24

Follow Annika Dev on Instagram @annika_poetry

I would like to dedicate this poetry collection
to all poetry lovers!!
—Annika

I have spread my dreams under your feet;
Tread softly because you tread on my dreams.
—W. B. Yeats

Contents

1. Why were they soulmates?
2. Yellow Candlelight
3. He wrote poetry
4. I write poetry because ...
5. My past was Golden
6. I wanted to write something
7. The way you speak
8. Betrayal
9. My favorite story
10. You want me back
11. Our promise to each other
12. Your world left with you too
13. My love for you ...
14. Time Remains
15. I will dream
16. Why do I love Poetry?
17. The wind blew yesterday
18. You made me fall in love with you
19. Stardust
20. Setting My Heart in Stone
21. Jade Green Leaves
22. The Rules
23. Dried Up Love
24. A Love Haiku

25	Woman Today
26	Dream within a Dream
27	Dreamers and Visionaries
28	True Love is Immortal
29	Of Life!
30	A Tale
31	Some Ruins Are Mesmerizing
32	There's a Thin Line Between…
33	Promises
34	The Wound
35	To: My Darling
36	Love
37	God is a Pimp!
38	Troubled Waters
39	I Was Good Once!
40	What's in A Name?
41	Let there be Love
42	The Shining Stars Above!
43	How Can I Ever Forget Your Smile? …
44	Her face: a dream
45	The Burning House
46	Imposter
47	A Happy Wanderer
48	Stuffed Pear
49	Lava
50	I Won!
51	My Narrative
52	Father
53	Shadows and Memories
54	Time is Poetry
55	What You Gave Me!

Why were they soulmates?

When they were alive
They searched for each other

Before they were alive,
While in the arms of death,
In their deepest slumber,
They dreamt of each other

Yellow candlelight
Golden colored
Illuminated evenings

General merriment,
chatty people abound
end of a hard, busy day
Some rest, followed by
cheerful hustle bustle

Medieval times, yes perhaps

Was this time, this light
and this atmosphere
the very birthplace,
Of fairy tales, magic, and romance?

He wrote poetry
His mind ached
If he didn't

His poems were tedious
They made you stare at pain
Face to face, reacquaintance
And you couldn't look away

I write poetry
Because it's my hiding place
And I don't want to be caught
Running away from things again

If you like mine, I feel like I've won
And if you don't
Nothing really matters, in the end

My past was Golden
and I didn't know it

Maybe it is God who decides
whose past
to truly lay to peace

Mine is still alive
and I won't let it die
it's not rotten and all dead
it's fresh and precious
and in my head

I wanted to write something
Truly wonderful and earth-shattering

So I burned my own blood
And started writing with it

It was an experiment quite successful
For instead of getting empty
I became fulfilled; happy

Your words
The way you speak
Seem like poetry to me

So does your silence

And the peace I feel
When I am with you
Is poetry too

Betrayal stinks foul

So, no more, fresh,
Fragrant Memories...

Memories of our
first puppy together, bouncing.
Sea side vacations
The mild scent of colorful
wild flowers

Memories of you, us
For me, not any more

Us going from
Total strangers
To true lovers

Is my favorite story

You want me back
As if you never broke my heart
I won't come back now,
not even once.
Not even in your dreams.

Our promise to each other
Of always being together
Remained unfulfilled . . .

But that doesn't mean
That we can't be one
In each others' dreams. . .

When you left me

your world left with you too

and now this realization

I loved being in it, one with you

My love for you
Would make
The rains
Look thirsty

My love for you
Would burn
Brighter than
The Sun

After it is all consumed
what still remains
is Time

Without ever catching
ahold of it
(that) which can be all lost
never to be found again

But what still remains
(to be grasped, yet again)
is Time

I shall dream a little . . . more

I will breathe a little . . . more

life into my dreams

Why do I love poetry?

It gave me answers
I thought I would never get
to important questions
now forgotten
And life lived, just like that
Carrying on, being unwhole and
limping almost, exhaustedly

Poetry, like a salve
has saved me
and my pained soul

The wind blew
A gentle breeze
Brushing against
My face softly

The Silver wind chimes
Tinkled sweetly

Was it you, my love
Who remembered me
Out of nowhere, suddenly...?

The way of love
The way of the world
How do they work?
Can someone let me know?

You made me fall in love with you,
Only to then, let me go

She was magic
made of stardust

he robbed her of it,
in the name of Love

only to find
an endless supply of it in her,

and now his hands shine
forever more

They love to tell me
how I should behave in Love

As if to some doll
pretty and dull

I revoke all the rules,
setting my heart in stone
and all my lovers, on fire!

Jade Green leaves
Icy cold Blue water
Feasting on it,
My eyes become cool, Green

There are rules
Then there are (some more) rules

Which ones 'rule' you the most?

(Alas), some rules, we all need!
Do, choose the best ones to succeed!

My love for you, has dried up
Like withered fallen leaves, on the ground
Which were once thriving and blazing Red

Yellow Sunflowers
your sunny disposition
my biggest grin

Let me make
my 'own' mistakes

Let me 'own' my mistakes

They will tell me
my worth,
what I truly deserve!

Do you remember?
When we had woken up together?
I recounted a dream to you
that you just had,
before waking up?
We smiled at each other
knowingly,
that smile would last an eternity
But,
a rude awakening;
I wake up today to discover
I had been dreaming...

Dreams are better than visions
dreamers, greater than visionaries
flawed dreams, when shattered
harm not many
flawed visions, when failed
injure many a soul!!

True love is immortal
So is one's soul

The soul's thirst
Is quenched only by God

And God's, only by Love

Hurt feelings
Hurt emotions
Hurt lines
make,
Heart lines
Blood lines
Blood veins
Blood streams
In my heart
Pain running Red
Traces the path
My heart,
What a bloody map,
Of life, love, you!

"I am an old man
wrinkly and frail
I dreamt though I am
a cuddly tiny babe.
Peering and smiling at me
with sweet loving care,
who you are, I want to
know, my dear?!"

"What are you babbling,
so sweetly about, baby?
O beautiful child of mine,
my dear sweet boy!"

Said the young mother
to her brand-new, bundle of joy!

Some ruins are mesmerizing!
The remains that they are,
their state of destruction
says a lot
about what once was!

Whole, pristine, untouched!

There's a thin line between
Love and Hate,
Life and Death,
Everything and nothing

Believe in promises
No more I do
Life didn't keep its word,
neither did you!

It's beautiful!
My wound!

Ruby Red, bloody jewels
On my heart, glinting,
In a squiggly pattern
An intricate, wonderful, design
It's a poem,
this wound!

My heart has taken
the pain given
by you, so well!!

To: My Darling

I was never chasing you
I was only chasing, what we had!
I hope you realize it too,
well enough before
you or I die!!

There was once a peaceful habitat
settled in my heart

But, then I fell in Love

A turbulent adventure
Not for everyone
Love is a calamity!!

Look at my heart now,
What a ruin!

God makes us sin
his decisions, lifelong, sting!

He makes us first, promising
the next best thing
gives us all the markings
and the makings of becoming
someone with greatness, striking!

And then, he takes it all
away, in a blink
(How *could* he do this to me?!)
Am I too not his offspring?

God is a pimp!

Troubled waters
Starry nights
Fluorescent dreams
Sleepless eyes
Elusive happiness
Hazy, me
Troubled times

I was good once
And God came to me
He left me though
For, I was always going to go bad, you see

I didn't like my name,
until you came along
Your name
Your love
only,
is worthwhile
I recognize myself
since I've loved you
Call me by your name

(This poem is for everyone who has loved, i.e. irrespective of their gender, orientation, race, color, etc.)

Let us all be filled with Love
When we talk,
when we look at others
Let there be Love everywhere!

(Don't let those dazzling
diamonds fool you so)

The shining stars above
sneakily made me believe

That there's fortune lurking
somewhere

And that, there's you

Still waiting for me

How can I ever
Forget your smile?
It made me keep
My heart safe, in you

Her face: a dream

serenity; gentle heaving
of her breasts; embodying
sunsets, sunrises
a calm sea
her mind; body
her face: a dream
come true

eyelids closed
endless mysteries
enclosed within

you would want to unlock

I am alive
in that one dot,
one spec,
one second

When all of the
house is burning down
around me
gulping (down) all that there is
surrounding me
alive or lifeless

But I am at peace although
I am about to burn next
I don't know how
else to live

I live for
That one second,
One eternity

Sometimes I feel
Like an utter fraud
An imposter
In my own life

But then
Shouldn't it be painless?
(And hurting not at all?)

You know life,
My heart,
And everything else

I am not in love
With any one of the aims
They want me to have

I may fall behind

Will always be at home
With myself though

A happy wanderer...

stuffed pear
stuffed bell pepper
a teddy bear, (stuffed)

this love and
other 'stuff'; fulfilling
tempting, telling

stuffed with
the happiness filling
that's us and life

full of meaning
nectar

Blazing red, hurting eyes
And burning in the throat

Still,

Drinking some fiery
Acid drink

Hoping to douse
the inner Lava

With more of the same

The moment I
started seeing myself
the way you did

I WON!!

You are the narrative I want to choose
The resolution to my inner conflict,
My elixir,

The one that I can't live without

Rinse your mouth
Five times at least
Especially after lunch and dinner
Told me, my father

They had a fight then
Him and mom that day
All night long
Going their separate ways
The next door dog was
on a barking tirade

No one cared for me as much
Ever again
Oh! And I cannot stand dogs
Ever since then

They say memories
Are like shadows

Pretty enticing
But not the real thing

(Cannot dwell too much on either
Although it's tempting)

They are alive though,
Always Hand in hand,
(One) with their master

time is a poem,
forever being written
it is poetry, in motion
always open
to interpretation
open to many interpretations
based on one's experience

time is ever new
and forever old
old; coz it forever was
and enchanting
coz it forever will be;
yet fleeting,
time is also magic

contained only by a few numbers,
still spilling over; this time
forever more, tricky; this time

when all the clocks stop working
time won't

and sometimes you wonder
even though the clock's working still,
why then,
time seems to have stood still

I started writing because of
what you gave me
was it heartbreak?
Or mind break?
Well, it was something!
Something did break
and not in a good way

There is no point to my writing
save for the lessening
of the heartache,
by the end of the day!

www.ingramcontent.com/pod-product-compliance
Lightning Source LLC
Chambersburg PA
CBHW061250040426
42444CB00010B/2336